What the River Says

What the River Says

Bijay Mahapatra

Translated by
Prof. Dr. Kamala Prasad Mahapatra

BLACK EAGLE BOOKS
Dublin, USA | Bhubaneswar, India

Black Eagle Books
USA address:
7464 Wisdom Lane
Dublin, OH 43016

India address:
E/312, Trident Galaxy, Kalinga Nagar,
Bhubaneswar-751003, Odisha, India

E-mail: info@blackeaglebooks.org
Website: www.blackeaglebooks.org

First International Edition Published by
Black Eagle Books, 2025

WHAT THE RIVER SAYS
by **Bijay Mahapatra**
Translated by **Prof. Dr. Kamala Prasad Mahapatra**

Original Copyright © **Bijay Mahapatra**
Translation Copyright © Kamala Prasad Mahapatra

All rights reserved. No part of this publication may be reproduced, stored in a retrieval system, or transmitted, in any form or by any means, electronic, mechanical, photocopying, recording or otherwise without the prior permission of the publisher.

Cover & Interior Design: Ezy's Publication

ISBN- 978-1-64560-740-3 (Paperback)

Printed in the United States of America

What the River Says

Contemporary Odia Poetry, unlike Poetry in other languages of India, exhibits a character that renders it untranslatable into a host language of non-sanskritic origin. The multiple openings, the verbal imageries, the inflections and the oralities subsumed by written words, often make it a translator's nightmare. In that sense Bijay Mahapatra is a difficult Poet to translate into English. I am delighted to see that Prof. Kamala Prasad Mahapatra in rendering BM's Poetry into English succeeds in tiding over most of the obstacles posed by the typical knots and chains in which the Poet spins his metaphor laden content, often leaving his intent shrouded, opaque or playfully halfdone. As a translator of repute and a Professor of English, KP knows only too well that the route to meaning in highly metaphorised poetry is bedevilled by allusions, and extrapolations not quite amenable to the discipline of the English Language. He gets over the glitz by overflying the intended, the implied and the conjectured by sticking to the literal. That infact is the route to reach the sensory subtext of fascinatingly illusory Poetry. Our thanks are due to both, the Poet and the Translator for setting this stage for us to show how the contemporary Odia poetry functions as a site for translation .

- **Haraprasad Das**
Eminent Poet

Poet Speaks

The journey from 'Bhrama Bhramana' to 'Gavira Hebaa Jae' has been quite thrillng, remarkable and memorable as well. The estuary of language leads the readers, critics, from the triviality of chaos to the sublimity of quietness making them traverse the tragectory of aesthetic ambience causing intermittent fatigue and ecstasy.

The lovers of poetry listen to poetry with deep pssion and insight. T. S. Eliot is right to observe 'genuine poetry can communicate before it is understood.'

The best poems have a way of making us feel something before we fully understnd, why or how it makes us feel this way. A good poem exists first of all as emotive, affective experience and then as an intellectual and analytical one.

Poetry has the capacity to be meaningful first at an emotive level before it is meaningful at analytic level. Poetry is certainly the portrayal of the landscape of pain and pleasure that one encounters in contemporary society.

The poet makes use of metaphors, images otherwise known as objective correlatives to reachout to the perceptive readers indirectly with his poetic vision.

I hope and trust that my translated poetry collection "What the River Says" shall receive the acclamation of the readers that will provide motivation to me to continue with the creative journey.

On this occasion I would like to express my hearty sense of gratitude and deep sense of indebtedness to the celebrated poet, Sj. Haraprasad Das, renowned translator Prof. Dr Kamala Prasad Mahapatra, Eminent writer Sj. Nityananda Panda, noted poet Sj. Arupananda Panigrahi.

I owe my heartfelt thanks to the Proprietor of "Black Eagle Books" Sj. Satya Pattanayak, his associate Sj. Ashok Parida for bringing out the book in record time.

I would like to thank all my friends, wellwishers and supporters for their unwavering support to accomplish my mission of writing poetry.

Jay Jagannath!

Bijay Mahapatra

Translator Speaks

The creation of any genre of literature is primarily based on three factors viz- Race, Milieu and Moment said renowned French critic Hippolyte Taine. Notwithstanding the pathbreaking revolution in cyberspace and information technology, literature remains unscathed being ensconsed on a farm saddle. Literature unwaveringly caters to the twin areas of human experience. It provides entertainment to de-stress life and enlightenment two illuminate the emotion and intellect, imagination and reason, realism and fantasy. The creative writer is a wizard to weave an aura of trust and conviction against the backdrop of make- believe landscape.

Translation is infact very much indispensable for a text in order to explore wider platform, larger clientele, wider canvas, universal accessibility and inclusivity. For serving this ambitious goal the international linguafranca, English is considered most suitable.

The tradition of translation and its wider practice

dates back to the sixteenth century Renaissance period, when the treasure trove of Greek and Latin literature used to be translated into English, French and Spanish and circulated worldwide. The thoughts, the ideas , the feelings, the passions, and the images presented in the work of the source language are represented in target language. Hence it is needless to say that translation has contributed in a significant way for the enrichment of world literature. Regional literature in India is also getting increasingly popular across the Globe, only due to the translation of the Classics and popular literature.

The job of a translator is crucial, sensitive and in a way herculean. He comes across many challenges during during the process in his bid to ascertain if he would translate,transliterate or transcreate the text without distorting the original content and intent reflected in the source language.

Against the backdrop of such assumptions and hypothesis,I have made a modest attempt to translate the Odia poetry collection "Gavira Heba Jae" of the renowned poet Sj. Bijay Mahapatra into English. Sj. Mahapatra makes use of myths, images, metaphors which are highly complex and intricate, drawn from the world of phenomenal reality blended with the situations of surreal world.

Efforts have been made to communicate Mahapatra's agony, anguish, angst and ecstasy are reflected in the source language.

If the translated poetry collection "What the River Says" unfolds new insights and causes ripples in charmed circle of incisive critics and discerning readers, I will feel that my endeavour is successful and goal is accomplished.

Sarve Bhabantu Sukhina Sarve Shantu Niramaya
Sarve Vadrani Pasyantu Maa Kaschit Dukh Vag Bhabet.
Om Shanti Shanti Shanti
Jay Jagannath

Kamala Prasad Mahapatra

Contents

Elephant or Man	15
Human	19
Come Let us Sleep here	20
Love it	21
Ridgeguard Flower	23
Defeat	25
Rat	26
Jaydrath	29
River	30
Horse Rider	33
The Wind	36
Saffron	37
Satyabrata	38
Now	48
Unchaste	51
Source	52
Nearer to Heart	54
Black Spider	56
Mother	58
Poet	59
Untouchable	61
Innocent	63
Eldest Son	65
Road	68
Tears	70
Kargil	71
A Word for Eccentricity	73
Old man	75
River Reverted	77
On Deepening	79
Stay where you are	88

Elephant or Man

(i)

What is there in the eyes
              to know who sleeps
                    on whose bed !

Fathers also look like
sons quite often
darkness may offer you blood
and that blood loses meaning
after hair disappears from head.

They had perhaps
left for respective homes
        causing ripples in river
might have laid their feet
on the last lake's address.

I remain as night
        of completed sleep
        concluded poem
Silent estuary of the past

Wild shrubs on the valley
their ecstatic breath of
inevitable credible cloud
some one has put as it were on my eyelids.

now vandalise loot
elephant turns human
human to elephant

No order he turn deaf
         at sacrificial soil
Weapons swept the river of blood
at the site of children's pyre.

When nothing was certain,
When truth could not be deciphered,
the reality from the illusion,
look alike or apparition
who could have died
elephant or the man.

Causes doubt
in Drona's mind
whether dead or alive.

       (ii)
Though lately I know
Kin assassin
is my touchstone.

Fire ball like dim moonlight
on the peak of wax or snow house beckoned me.
(iii)
May be sound of Silence
morning dews of Cocacola drink
citizens from Indraprastha to Hastina
                      becomes Spirits
as river knows not speed
letter knows not address
weapon hardly knows the target
nor the taste of war field
sour or saline.

I wonder
it's beyond my reach
how five minors
remained in deep slumber?

my germs were excited
        in the impatient quiver
how name or image got upset

From that day abrupt tears
on whose order become abysmally soft
                like changed clothes .

affection collected for you
on the anger ridden palm of creator
                    is not rice

soft unfelt
jaundiced approach
fake play or empty lap
    of a lifeless snow toy

For that avoided trodden path
fell on untrodden path
didn't knock the iron door
immerged under night's mercy
fondled a tuft of grass with pain balm
confusing life
fed a capricious milching cow.

Human

No, nothing
amid the hollowness
             of a dictionary
humans have a noiseless discipline !

vocal bird understands nothing
hears stonified words
            from historic Pushpagiri caves
makes out own voice
who is it? asks
keep the door open
keep open womb fire
keep preserved
the arrogance of high rampart
                with the sacred sound
                        of fire harp
                in the heritage Kingdom
                of valiant warrior!

Come Let us Sleep here

Let us lie down here
by spreading the necklace of internal strife.
step _ sons can't be Poets
come, let us shrink our limbs
dream like a fish entwined
     . in the net of half death.

How shameful my introduction with you !
you had hands legs like me
eyes were transparent like september sky
words in my voice were
more smooth than your signs
Still my creative mind
used what language for which
family is construed as sainthood
Life is viewed as sickness of cough,
come let us sleep here
under the independent triumphant flag
         of so called gloom
Come we will sleep.

Love it

Love your body adorned
              on mahogany bed
also love your
nectar coated wheatish body
with coastal productivity
my thoughts feelings
              are suffocated.

breaths of life
are a decent sail
on the passionate
waters of youth.

I love your funeral ashes
love passionately your
blood stained clothes
            like a loyal wasp
love your attractive structure

overwhelmed in the preface
      to see a few people like
donkeys disloyal to paternity

I hardly ignore
rather meet and hug

I am the first horse
ordered to lie on burial ground
no distinction for me
if palate is delectable or contemptible
　　　　　with taste or distaste
suffering is inferno
or anodyne in heaven
my dance reflects isolation from blush
in cadence rhythm of lyricism
like a hurt bride !

I love you
since remote past
with funny chemistry
　　　of attraction
and repulsion
our relation
is intriguing
sometimes reaches
zenith of Joy
other times rots in hell .

Ridgeguard Flower

No one hears
if nothing
is audible
to any one
mild strike
of special tears
suppressed anger
of dormant volcano
how long shall
cause fog
in the dreamy
sky of memory ?

I am same landmark
      very much alone
       within you
       alone you
I am your claw
the crazy
dice stick
of your
generous ribs

bits and scraps
of my letter
slips in aerial
uncertainity of wind
in eunuchism of words
      by eccentrics
amid gap of horse rider's
illustrious devotion
I collapse beside your beauty
like ridgeguard flowers
that pale in morning.

Defeat

Tabor was unaware
that defeat evolves
from any other finger
whose percussion
resonates to burst
the door of skin open
gruelled from inside
as it were a bier
of friend foe imbroglio
with pyre burning inside heart.

I reminisce
in nostalgia
how much passion
was there but now
romance passion
sweet away
making platform clean
Come my vanquished son
       on elephant back
       to see the honey layer
receded in phases.

Rat

(i)
Not able to
dig soil since
many days
not able to
display ecstasy
with tit bits
either at home
or anywhere outside
not swam in the sea
        for long
not even built
the bridge to connect
not dug hole
on river bank
measuring with moustache
my limbs have shortened
with the rags of body hair
with the precious touch
of soothing breeze
hope burns spreads
        like wild fire
never bothers to stop.

(ii)
Reminisce delectable
palate of
rice water dry fish
rustic glass ball games
amid dust and dirt
smear of sweet past
flees away causing mystery .

My hairy body fails
to contain the pain
or the mirage of sweat
amid the depth of hair
I simply move backward

stand looking at the flowing river
near coconut tree of backyard
where all are flown away
even things stronger
       than dreams
in the labour room
of the twigs.

(iii)
Seen minutely
of course nothing is flown away
the jungle of wild shrubs spinach
sweet aggression
of honey bees

in our broken
tile thatched house
nothing is lopsided
not even the whisper
      of spring
on the grey beards
reciting the hymn
of advancing maturity.

Further think over to myself
I am instrumental
to remove barricades
beckon flood water
amid midnight silence
seasons are always welcome
          to my house.

May it be rains
on sun's sizzling heat
resilience of spring
or revelry of summer festivals
all seasons suit me
   to hide warmly
amid winter clothes
to portray the rhythm
    of grating noise.

Jaydrath

Memory is brazen lie,
may be rain passes off
quietly like
the arrogant silence
        of bare tree
studded with bones
that only back tracks
persuasive pretentions
darkness illusory
contrived Jayadrath evening.

Language now a days
is such loyal follower
it is wellnigh difficult
to know the direction that
water of penitence flows
your flowing locks wavy hair
generate fragrant passion of spring
            or exude inferiority
        by niggardly emission.

River

(i)
There is little difference
between river and water.
you are a river

I am inebriated sailor
navigating in your water,
watch crimson colour of morning sun
reflecting on the soft smooth
budding banyan leaves
along with shed furs
of agile chirping
birds in their nests.

If I were stuck in depth of
some one's navel
or in the dental ridge
of maiden snake
I won't have let you
flow as river.
(ii)
What will river speak ?
on itself

river never
makes discrimination
own purse
courtyard home
littered with
rat's teeth

glittering rays
of setting sun
river has nothing to say.

This like floats like sweat smell of
sage Bharat's holy jug
floats incessantly amid tidal waves
            in the whirlpool
                of indifference

What will river speak
while controlled
by fathomless whirlpool?
absolute autonomy
            was better
no restriction
on free movement
any time as per preference
draw plan to wriggle out
of mundane pursuits
of turmoil tumult despair

Bed is there
near water source
bed brings sedation
lulls to sleep
sleep helps remove
all agonies
ushers into
an arena of breathtakingly
calm plenitude
leaving worldly worries
far away beyond sight.

Horse Rider

(i)
Like ascending descending
the anguish of defeat
is felt by the horse
of the chariot
of valiant Vikramaditya
pain of living
in this world
is like the pain
of festering sore
amid the canvas
of journey and salvation
woven rosy dreams
to the orbit of abyss
holding on to the penelope
of yours and your passion
behaved obstinately
       with horse
making beards perfumed
like alloy of Pellets
I have absorbed sleeplessness.

Why no one is seen
nor did any one see
only saw deep blue water
        of Shyama Kund
excellent cadence
of rudratala
that joins
earth with heaven
buy its wonderful rhythm
sometimes by the
intoxicating fragrance
        of flowers
garland falls down
I am excited
Wrapping up
the iceberg
and feel the
spring of joy.

No matter
if hands changed
touch changed
words change
amid quietness
still Sumitra
the charioteer
of Abhimanyu
navigates on the

sands of tears
to dip it into soil.

(ii)
Your habit is
to stand stretching hands
near thirst
the thirst only dies
amid the sweat
of nose ring
or rain and thunder

Thirst is visible
on the bony
hunch backed
humans cutting across
age groups
sleeps blissfully
with a maid's body.
touch nudge fondle
the lack of trust
unveil the flower bed
      of conscience
time is ripe
to raise your
secret sword.

The Wind

Cautionary three lines
are not drawn
for that
the youth of
doors and windows
is not safeguarded
from immoral advances of thieves
Oh ! characterless wind
by nudge nullified clouds
made you listen holy songs
      of fairies through
      the flute hole of spine.
burnt you in south fire
swept away from shameless nostrils
your silkworm's
concentration from
tabla and
song's rhythm
silence of words
broke the furnace
even now my feet
causes rhythm
in the hot cauldron
      of emotions,
Oh ! wind
blow at least once as zephyr
amid the hilly terrains of words.

Saffron

What can the stone
leaned against sorrow do
wild wind blows
though cracks
      of despised cheeks or lips
which saffron
funeral pyre
moves carelessly
to engulf all ?

What if
the blackhooded oriole
comes painted with
fulsome yellow colour
sings in classical
Kalahansa kedar rhythm
washing away all stigmas
glorifying ancient Kalinga
crazy seedlobes
rush like grey hounds
amid floral festiveness
I would slip into
abyss of barbarism.

Satyabrata

(i)
Some are blinded
being mistaken for
telling absolute truth

Truthful people can not
teach lessons
of humility
to spirits
nor have they
potential to
mystify with
magical chants
in moonlit evening
they dive into the
labyrinth like the fog
which continues perpetually
          at a place
where unwrapped
appears wrapped
Tamala flower tails
    to know there
Pairs with locked hands

are in love or conflict
Staying beside
auspicious water filled pitchers
or unpronounced
black serpent
of darkness.

(ii)
No one knows
how the world will appear.
may be round like orange or apple or egg
sin's appearance
or a sheer illusion
like spider's smooth cobweb

This world is like
      a leaning ship
         overloaded with merchandise
sailing overseas countries
that has set its voyage
on auspicious Kartik purnima
the world looks like
Satyabrata 's tummy

(iii)
Flowers perhaps don 't like
to be prisoners in garden
          like Satyabrata

They are aware
of brittleness
      of flowers and leaves
      few dew drops
      damage them
things are destined
to changes transformation
beauty is ephemeral
no use to grieve
over the pimples on face.

Soldiers disappear
in to the sloping
abyss of village
look from a distance like saree clad
women in state of romance.

(iv)
Oh God ! I wish
you had made
my sombreness sorrow flow down
              as fragrant oil
              from my eyes,
I won't have
demanded fulfilment
through children's success
or safe haven for self.

(v)
Wind blows carelessly
bringing in sizzling aroma
you are there
with your unseen
arrogance being
immune to changes
like blue lines drawn
by wind on water surface.

(vi)
Unrestrained pleasure
sometimes turns into
blue lagoon of sorrow.
tears hardly subdue
heat of body once more.

I keep my feet
beside such sharp
weapon of truth
that I turn into
melted moonlight
    of dew drops.
(vii)
Palm treated
as eyes is made
to swim across
the junction with
stained lid

Sun is shaken
amid black night
with sweet fragrance
blood gets stirred
amid dark clouds
on the river side
I am afflicted asthma
of focused moonlit night
not visible if flying
half mast or high mast.
how long shall I
appeal to sensitive
masters of words
with duplicate images?

It's like
bombardment
without noise
weapon without hand
bubble without water flow
I am epitome of unresolved tomfoolery
wild new moon night
devoid of elegant linens or embroideries.
(viii)
Is closure of eyes
not sign of love
does disapointment
of thirst not beckon
      the Red Sea ?

Is silence
of unuttered sound
not better than groaning
does the ash not
offer palmful greenery
through drumstick branch?
now feel like
getting transformed at midnight
into half made deities.
arrow on the cute bow
wins over illusion
void assured me
of blue sky
peepal buds
promised me
      flowers of anguish
spring assured of
sweet redolent breeze ;
hardly do I know
if the remaining portion
         of my life
         is pawned
      with whirlpool of
sorrow or joy
with black hair or
      grey hair
This much
I know
my sorrow sleeps

like a forlorn witch
amid nucleus
of lotus flower
in a state of cold.

(ix)
Mom said this time
holding my hand
this hand is not mine
this feet is
of fathomless road
eyes are of
the circular sky
I said thoughtfully
my children are
of which flowers
of what saffron nucleus
or of what fragrant
    petals of wind?

I also said
tears roll down
    my eyes
I have not been able
to stop it so far
with any stone of strength.

He said
tears are to be

burnt like demon
extending upto heaven
where light is lit
darkness under the lamp
sleeps quietly there !
(x)
At the children's
pilgrimage of bloody river
it was not possible
to control myself
vision wished
to become invisible

blood wished
to be red dye
in lake water
on the picturesque bank.

My strength
was not recognised
in seven islands
lotus did not bloom
at my feet
no pretext
became unavoidable
south wind of Ashok flower
asked for tips to
sensitive grey hairs
        of ears.

It's not river
a semicolon
my pain is defeated
by rotten stinking smell
of Ketaki flower,
nothing is beautiful here
only sprawling darkness
      like blue serpent
on a death trap
for unlucky people.

(xi)
As the length of
the opening saree
did not suffice
I stood with folded hands
joined the knees
to form a firm knot
that will not open abruptly
without getting
usefulness of eyes
closed eyelids

Lest it should not
suffice I shed shame
stretched both arms
      to my lover.
for eyes only
man has to

stand with humiliation.
who asked
to forget
right path
grant me
fear of fog
unconditional death
on Siali creepers
shape bodies
in series
one after the other
so that one
will regret
in old age
to notice
black mole
of vibrant youth.

Now

Numerous palmbuls
beside hand
road was there
    for feet
river was there
    for water
sky of eyelids was there
for bluish green landscape
that was intensely passionate
for intoxicating clouds
of ensuing seasons.

Now eyes are not
said to be eyes
mind is not
compulsively picked like flowers
from the abyss of
    great trust
now clouds are dormant
like cigarette smoke remain as remnants of
abandoned dreams.

Nothing like blame or discredit

limbs hands legs
are monitored
by dictates of hunger on wants
above all
mature minds
tend to acquire
indiscipline
like seasoned
banyan tree.

Roots are too old
to look for
river stream
bat's noise
jackal's bark

Lone star of sky
will not look for
old romantic lovers.
after things
fall silent
which words
trigger warmth in me
am I that eternally
aspired banyan tree anxiously
awaiting evening strangers?

Whole of Jambu island
contains rains,

wind is not wild
like in the past
body seems dry
lacks lustre
what page
will you open now
oh ! the vocal one?

Unchaste

while stepping out
             of home
wind flaps two wings
widow moonlight
unleashes
thick pitch darkness
on the river bank
of strained relation

on the rain water
of womanhood.
chaste unchaste
distinction blurs like
forlorn footsteps of rest life on seabeach
gradually losing identity.

Source

Come now
will go hand in hand
    to river bank
will shed the scale
beat the chest
wriggle out of
unwarranted mess
like transformed
dacoit Ratnakar
emerging from
termite mound
as the arrow is
released from bow,
milk released
from cow's breast
come like flocks
of plain paper furs
flying hither and thither
shall be written
on us in letters of all colours
in all states.

The manner in which
pumpkin tree creeps in
beak pecks the egg shells
like the ink of blood
sprayed on shirt
we will proceed
with warmth
anointing the pains
with ointment.

Nearer to Heart

I have to
go to you
if not today
may be tomorrow
of course don't know
what struggle is involved
in ascension or descension
wearing or changing
embroidered apparel
wading across
blowing wind
on bending like moss
on any new stream.

Then it's to be
understood that
foot and palm
have hardly
any language
as eyes donot
have language
so you need not
    write in ink

don't have to
aim the arrow
on the wordless eyeballs
on the stinking
body of any fish.

Amid the sweat smell
of abdominal hair
or tortured as throat bump
in the hawan tray
of filial love
I am a musical instrument
not able to know if
I am grinded turmeric
        of hot noon

Or black hooded oriole
embroiled suffocated
in the whirlpool
heart getting
repeatedly stunned.

Black Spider

(i)
You never gave anything
           took away everything
Snatched flowers
tightly studded
on the black braided hair
           fun and frolic
           from red lips

raided all treasure
           with sweat of theft
           caused gruelling pain
and left only
a few wild flies
           tainted signs
on the soft suave cheeks

(ii)
Home is indeed a trap
while inside one is doomed
going out is prone
           to attack,
Placating many dreams

I have learnt
        to build house
and preserve sorrows
        from honey bees
learnt to play
on the swing
with thin muslin threads
moving the limbs
        since childhood
while emerging
from anaesthetic fluid
created a trap of bonding

Mother

Saves everything
whatever comes her way
drives away snake
from cowdung cake heaps
instils maturity wisdom
              into grassy soft childhood
motivates to fight
      with legendary lawyer Madhubabu,
she is afraid of
              sending us out
we get back home in evening
like fish lured to fish hook.

Poet

You have not been effective
        so far to welcome salute
never showed any excitement
words are always anaemic
        helpless, lacking in direction !

Woman is fine
till her modesty sustains
garland of self choice ceremony
    shakes impatiently
     to explore the ocean of uncertainty
no peak is visible then
mercilessness engulfs
        like the hearse.

you fondle, kiss
weave tapestry of love
you never indulge in
rehearsal of human touch
     through accumulated
    sweet amid my hairs
you only pierce with
sulfur wick of fire colour
    you approach on pleasant

  evenings with sleepy eyes
to tell
colour of blood
    is indeterminate
like extralunar month.

Untouchable

Making plans to enter
apparently hungry indigestion
ancestry feets sidelined, neglected
making attempt to appear

Lying neglected so long
getting restricted by strong force
of distance still showing
      innate confidence
looks like dimmed red lily
attempts to make it more red
stir the static stars
autumnal dry shrubs
rejuvenate fallow lands
makes apparent bid to enter,

That untouchable
wild mule
bridge of
light and darkness
hot noon of
the tropical state
it is opportune time

for Aswini Kumar's entry
in the lap of
dying mother.

Innocent

No one can be blamed
portrayal of star
is more serious
         than our thought
strike of night
         is heavier
         than disbelief
don't know if it is foolish to think
                 where leads
                 the ladder
       to mesmerising heaven.

Oh ! night I am prematurely pregnant
stay away
        from my darkness
I don't need
           nectar of your tongue
           nor milk from grains
I feel in intensity of bones
the blood pressure of
                  the flute bearer

stable yet noisy
which blessed hand of goddess
     disappears like
    unlucky lines
is there any sight
without caption
   more delicate than eyes?

Eldest Son

(i)
He would hate
emerged from
      the womb of queen
      with fragrance of flower
I would have tied
      like a talisman
and become dearer
      like the past
        on Ahalya stone

I won't have
compromised, made adjustments
      with musical evening
oblation to god's idols

I am valorous
Sabyasachi
amid petals of coloured flowers.
If I had the
eldest son
would have
named Prabhanjan

　　　　　in class three
would not have
asked his mother
with white sandalwood paste
　　　to go near
auspicious banyan,Kalpabata
　　　　to wish for something
may ignore
　　　　　incense but
let him come once more with coupling knot
　　　　before evening descends down.

He comes unexpectedly before the knot loosens
makes age hollow
turns the sculpted space
　　　　　　　on queen's cheek
　　　　　　　inexpressible

The state in which
　　　mercury drips
　　　from vagina
how could he
survive amid noise
how could he
sleep with broom
　　　　under head
without attending
to letter
reached in the evening?

(ii)
You are
every day
an additional
exaggerated
nameless name
scent dipped
fragrant hanky
and the lifeline
      of my maiden struggle.

You are small
bamboo stick
      useful for field
you are the
exertion first word
      for wound
your childhood nudity
      is epitome of purity.

Road

If I were
a muddy road
the sign of
      your car wheel
      would have remained
      on any last conversation.

Just very recently
I have fallen
in love with
honest rains
on the earthen pot
      of my eyes
let them come
    in form of tears
    as harbinger of death.

I am a communicative
          voice that
          reflects pains
unleashing irony
    like child widow
    having menstruation ;

Oh! god
make me
at least a road.

Tears

Asked the progressive clouds
wondering in sky
the meaning of tears
just enquired the meaning
torrential rain
        of opportune time
halted just like
        confession of woman's love
        to her aged husband
got stuck in the cerebrum
        like the string of piano.

Kargil

(i)
I know you want
to return to your
        native place
intend to draw
demarcation with flag symbol
                  of your state
just make the river
of patriotism flow
in our arteries.

(ii)
Want to steal soil
want to predominate
        over the dying stream
        to collect some flowers
or pluck it from
        someone's entwined hair knot
and throw it
        into polluted water
        of Sindhu river
        as a spiritual slave?

(iii)
You ask your grand pa
how kept fragrant
rajanigandha
under the blanket
      on honeymoon night.
many Vaidehis come from under the plough
      of poor smoke ploughman to enjoy
          the swing during Raja Festival
ask them where and
why boundary of
humanity is in Kargil on Kashmir !

Produce music
      on bamboo flute
or else engage
      in measuring
      mountain's peak,
stop firing bullets
reminisce the past
in company of grandpa
Sacred thread alongside
sacramental beard
aroma of Rajanigandha
rather settle to sleep
      in Kargil.

A Word for Eccentricity

I think
it would have been
better not to have
．．．．．．．．．．spoken anything.
if I had turned
eccentric ignorance
．．．．．．into only dreaminess
．．．．．．to ensure smooth release
in stead of
little tongue getting stuck
it wouldn't
have been proved
that Poets are
Viswamitras each.

Own horse is
．．．．．．not always under control
aromas do not spread
．．．．．．with flower's sweet will
armlets and bangles
break under duress

the silence of embrace
tickle the sensation
remove all pains
cleanse the dustbin of sorrows.

Old man

Everything could be
                done now
fairies could be
won in illusion
penance could be
offered to setting sun
amid palm forest gaps
letters of friendship
or enmity could be sent
                to the moon or butterflies
all will come
as blankets and shawls
                to offer warmth
                of some more winters
amid the company of
                sons daughters
and Jokes humor
of grand children,
flow dreamily
                like a river
the air coming out
                of funeral pyre

seems to stitch
           the cracked palm leaves.

Everything is possible now
even with weakened bones
can buy dice board
to Draupadi of Mahabharat

Some may sit near head
some at the feet
some in the lap
        to use as washroom ,
some may suggest
affix your thumb impression
           to transfer property
if you can't write
everything is possible now.

River Reverted

Address of rain
may be asked to
      fallen buds
rebellious leaves
different looking
meaningful candle
resembling the
uninterrupted sunlight
of the unknown sky.

I would have
preferred to hit
a stone and
fall like tears
and getting up in a flash
      as a woman,
sunlight should have
appeared along with
      water fire
smears of blood
like parrot's beak
      after that flowed.
as a river

by swallowing
stone embankment
      of Sebei Santara
made with the bone's sweat
         of many generations.

After a few years
some ice cubes
can be collected
from old beloved's
choked voice

To treat the feet swollen
after climbing mountain
after some rains
mature fish
being separated
      from kids
    shall get into
    Magunia's
stay in mud sand slush
in the prison of
greed and attachment
suffer untold misery.

On Deepening

(i)
Shall we wrap up
careless joy
      with the penelope
      of obliging beloved
      to dive deep into
one another's
      pain and pleasure ?

As the flowers
          are upset, disturbed
          in dingy isolated room
God's hand is not so long
          to check tears
and decimate voice built by it.

Once I stood
under a banyan tree
and at Konark
where sun rays
      fall first
stood with own diversities

sometimes near water
sometimes got
submerged in deluge water
remained in the
lap of some
        like Radha
        in emptiness,
at times became
weapon of star war
fell victim to
betrayal
became a killer
   in Kargil
turned into moon
when the wounds
appeared deeper.

(ii)
With more depth
suffering becomes
long shadow of rains

On the pan of
midnight tingling bangles
cake, is tasteless
amid the tussle
of daughter in_ law
mother in_ law going deeper
quarrelsome sister in_ law

appears lost in
invincible wishes.

This had to happen
           every year
who knew
      that you would be
         in the other side
while crossing river

You may not be there
shrubs and creepers
might be haunted
           by your spirit
like goat or unknown frightened snake
                hiding in tree hole
before the advent
       of deluge
above all
outside the newmoon
   of suffering
    getting centralised
           as a storm
would have stood
           with a flute
           lured into
           your thirst
        in persuasive tone,

What happens when
              is not known
I sneak into
the lanes of
your wounds
like a fox
obstinate bee
with its blindness
remains imprisoned
              inside flower

Sleep becomes deep
in the village by_ lanes
the last part
of your sentence
becomes grave
in slow indistinct voice.

(iii)
Dawn breaks
amid searching for
              cigars
with the sleeping pills
      for deep sleep
my mother
wears green
sleepless look ,

Proceeding a little ahead

my uncle's house
        at Rajnagar comes
reminds my childhood
mischief of dipping legs
        in water during boat ride,
Papa keeps an eye
on mom's payal
drowning in river,
matter was
to delve deep
water caused havoc
I make futile exercise
like election every year
like growing age of girls
through generous foams.
now there is less sleep
        less poems

Tears have
weakened the sting
it's not possible
to go anywhere
my potential needs
    to be deepened.

(iv)
Boundary stayed
in its original place
ditch is filled

        with some water
stones have
gathered moss
wild grass have
grown across
        the narrow murrum road
recognised the torn flag
at a distance
getting back consciousness.

Whatever was written
in the rhythm of wind
began to flutter
against the boundary
words make trumpet.

Chirping of baby bird
              not heard
              not mature
        to break the shell
time is not ripe
to move the finger
in the bird nest of anxiousness
nothing is broken or burnt
with wrong eyebrow movement,
Boundary is in its place.

(v)
I cut off from my body
the feathers of age
      by calculating myself
as I have to go
on some mountain's seat
to put letters of my
      ancestors on auspicious leaf
chance to reach heaven
albeit turning into a dog.

Rubbed further
sharpened like pencil tip
cats brushed teeth
with fish bones
snakes of various kinds
shed their scales
in their own style,
I set out to my home
after shaving myself.

(vi)
Loafer boy
makes love
on internet
says I don't know
who is father
who is brother
what is home

what is fear
now complaining
about writing Poetry.

New theory has
        come up in town
how so ever one is bald.
cheeks are shrunken
His poetry
shall be plump
like potbellied Ganesh

now a days the poets
with elephant trunks
have sprouted tales
and they consider it
        as roots
loafer boys
        are found tonsured,
Cuckoos are chirping
on roads pan shops
and tea stalls
leaving behind mango buds

Cymbalists are
strategically fitting
Bhima Bhoi's Poems
into the cymbals
of their stories and Poems.

What does the
loafer boy know
how much deep
the roots get
amid the sand
and stone gaps
on the apparently
Stagnant waters
of Jobra canal,
the song emerging
    from the rhythmless
    broken trumpet
out of sheer anguish
how can loafer boy
understand the
degree of pleasure
on the panty clad
or jeans clad broken body !

Out of heap of termites of hypocrites
Valmiki has emerged
    at several places
    in native and foreign countries
poison comes out of fangs of
    nonvenomous snakes,
Palash flowers have bloomed
loafer boy hardly spoils sleep
dreams to see the words
bear Poetic cadence
in the limbs of Partner.

Stay where you are

Stay there
who so ever
is any where
mountains rivers
shrubs creepers
be loyal for
certain time,
wait for
     the opportune time
stay quiet
Palm leaves
lips stay sweet
amid stubborn wind
Sribatsa has not
laid his foot
on my chest
in night time.

Jewel still needs time
to appear red ,
body is not heavy
procession is yet to start
blackhooded oriole has

not made any pledge
auspicious diya
is yet to be sanctified
in the premises of Goddess
Bhabini is not yet ready ,
be there where you are

Not much peach
           is visible
               on your pedicured feet ,
Parrot has not made prophecy
mongoose is not intoxicated
until it hugs
the wet body of fish
children are immune
to any external strike
birth place is not abandoned
as yet , Goddess
be there wherever
you are.

Black Eagle Books

www.blackeaglebooks.org
info@blackeaglebooks.org

Black Eagle Books, an independent publisher, was founded as a nonprofit organization in April, 2019. It is our mission to connect and engage the Indian diaspora and the world at large with the best of works of world literature published on a collaborative platform, with special emphasis on foregrounding Contemporary Classics and New Writing.

www.ingramcontent.com/pod-product-compliance
Lightning Source LLC
Chambersburg PA
CBHW060621080526
44585CB00013B/926